D1203267

HOW?D THEY DO THAT?

in...

COLONIAL AMERICA

Mitchell Lane

PUBLISHERS

P.O. Box 196

Hockessin, Delaware 19707

HOW?D THEY DO THAT?

in...

Ancient Egypt

Ancient Greece

Ancient Mesopotamia

Ancient Rome

The Aztec Empire

Colonial America

Elizabethan England

The Mayan Civilization

The Persian Empire

Pre-Columbian America

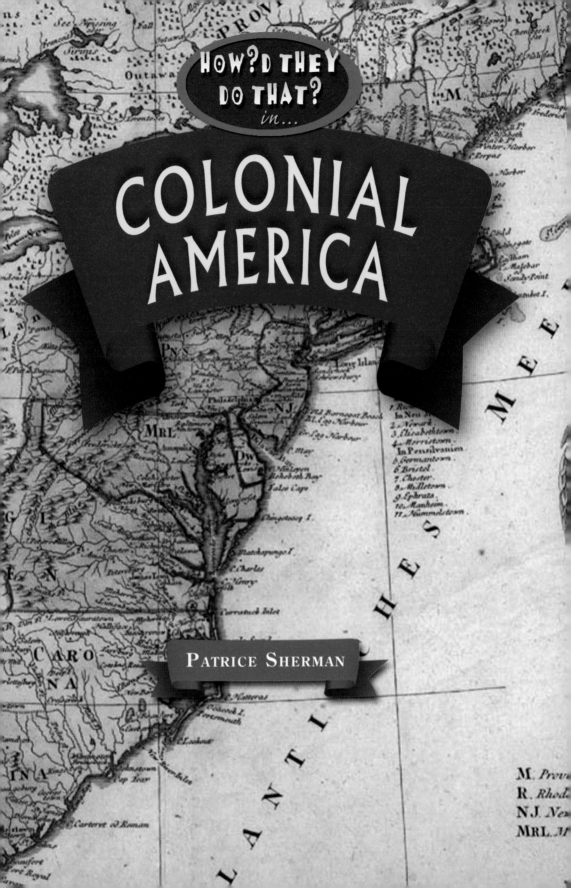

HOW?'D THEY DO THAT?

in...

COLONIAL AMERICA

PATRICE SHERMAN

Copyright © 2010 by Mitchell Lane Publishers, Inc. All rights reserved. No part of this book may be reproduced without written permission from the publisher. Printed and bound in the United States of America.

Printing   1   2   3   4   5   6   7   8   9

Library of Congress Cataloging-in-Publication Data
Sherman, Patrice.
  How'd they do that in colonial America / by Patrice Sherman.
      p. cm. — (How'd they do that?)
  Includes bibliographical references and index.
  ISBN 978-1-58415-817-2 (library bound)
  1. United States—Social life and customs—To 1775—Juvenile literature. 2. United States—History—Colonial period, ca. 1600–1775—Juvenile literature. I. Title.
  E188.S546 2010
  973.2—dc22

                                                                        2009001298

PUBLISHER'S NOTE: This story is based on the author's extensive research, which she believes to be accurate. Documentation of such research is contained on page 60.
    The internet sites referenced herein were active as of the publication date. Due to the fleeting nature of some web sites, we cannot guarantee they will all be active when you are reading this book.

                                                                        PLB

CONTENTS

Hopewell finished lacing up the front of her dress and tied on her apron. A thin, pale light shone through the crack between the shutters. Swiftly, she slid back the wooden bolt that held them fast and pushed them open. The sun was already above the horizon. Leaning over the sill, she took a deep breath of spring air and wrinkled her nose. Instead of smelling sweet bayberry and meadow rose, she got a big whiff of boiling potash lye and goose fat. It was soap making day.

Hannah, their indentured servant, had already built a fire in a pit of rocks outside and put the great iron cauldron on to boil. Hopewell would help her stir it until the lye and grease had simmered down into a brown syrupy liquid. After it cooled, they would pour it into a large iron-staved barrel to be ladled with a dipper whenever they need some soap.

Hopewell sighed. Soap making was hot, tiresome work. She was thankful they only had to do it once a year.

SOAP MAKING AT BAYBERRY COVE

"Ezra! Come back!" she heard her sister Patience shout.

Hopewell spied her three-year-old brother in his pinafore dress toddling as fast as he could straight toward the fire pit. Two long lead strings attached to his shoulders flapped like ribbons streaming in the wind. Without stopping to put on her cap, she sped from the bed-chamber, leaped over the back threshold, and dashed across the kitchen garden. "Ezra!" She grabbed the lead strings, yanking so hard he fell on his bottom and howled.

"You have to hold on all the time so he will not wander abroad." She hoisted him up and handed the end of the leads to Patience. "That is why he has strings on his dress."

"But I only let go for a moment to pick up my distaff." Patience waved a stick on which she had bound a thick bundle of sheep's wool.

"Then tie his strings to your own apron while you pull thread," Hopewell told her.

Though she was only five years old herself, Patience had to mind the baby all day while their mother was busy with cooking and weaving. Suddenly Hopewell felt glad she had the soap making to attend to, for sometimes keeping her little brother out of mischief seemed the hardest work of all.

Inside the house, her mother ladled out cornmeal pudding for breakfast. They all sat on wooden benches at the pine board table and ate from wooden bowls with wooden spoons.

"Remember to put your cap on, daughter," her mother reminded her. Hopewell was eleven—old enough to have to keep her head covered like a young lady.

She slipped the starched white bonnet with its wide curved brim over her head and tied a bow beneath her chin. For a moment she wondered what she looked like. She had never seen her own face. Her father, who traveled to Boston, told her that people there had things called looking glasses or mirrors in which they could see themselves. He also told her that when her grandmother was a girl back in the 1680s, mirrors had been banned in Bayberry Cove because the church sextons feared they would encourage vanity. Now, however, it was 1725 and families could purchase many things her father called "modern." Glass windows, for instance.

He had promised to bring back glass panes for the windows when he finished with his trading in Boston. Then they would be able see outside all winter instead of keeping the shutters closed against the cold. Hopewell liked the idea of having windowpanes, but not as much as having a looking glass. Perhaps her father could bring that next.

"'Tis time you got here," Hannah said crossly, when Hopewell finally returned to the cauldron. "Did you bring the salt?"

Hopewell had no idea what she was talking about. "Do you mean to salt the soap like venison stew?" She laughed.

Hannah stopped being cross and laughed, too. "Your mother said I could teach you how to make the soap cake."

Cakes of soap? That sounded almost as strange to Hopewell as a looking glass.

Hour after hour they stirred the pot of soap, singing rounds to make the time pass more quickly. At last Hannah let a drop of soap cool and placed it on her tongue to taste it. "It stings but doesn't burn," she said. That meant it was ready for salting.

Hopewell's mother brought the salt box out to them, and Hannah began to scatter fistfuls of salt into the pot. To Hopewell's amazement, the soap started to froth. Peaks of foam rose up like the crests of ocean waves. She and Hannah scooped this foam out and smoothed it into a big wooden pan.

Hopewell looked at the nearby bayberry bushes and had an idea. She plucked some leaves and pressed them into the hardening soap, making a pattern. "Now it will smell sweet," she said. "And look fine, too."

Patience came out with Ezra to see what they had done. Hopewell was pleased by how firmly Patience held Ezra's strings to make sure he didn't get near the fire.

Patience admired the new soap. "It looks as good as gingerbread." At the word *gingerbread*, Ezra tried to take a bite, and they had to pull him back again.

"Don't fret," their mother told them. "Perhaps I will make ginger-bread tomorrow to mark our good news." She pulled a folded sheet of paper with a red wax seal from the pocket   of her apron. "The post rider came with a letter from your father. His trading has gone well. He is coming back with glass windowpanes. And something else." She glanced at Hopewell.

"A looking glass?" Hopewell asked.

"Yes."

"'Tis a marvel!" Hopewell clapped her hands. "I cannot wait to see it." And, she thought, her own face, too.

This photograph was probably taken around 1900, but the house is much older and very similar to a colonial house. The sloping roof is covered with closely fitted wooden shingles that kept the house warm in the winter and dry when it rained.

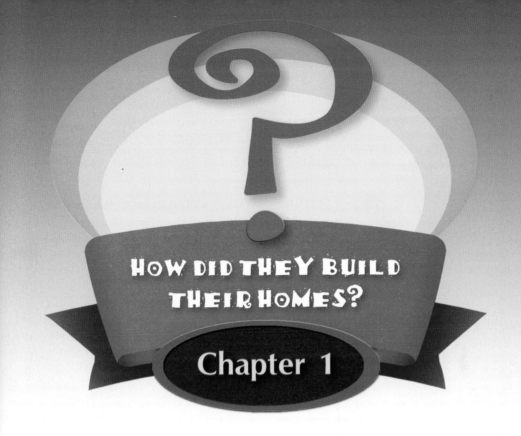

HOW DID THEY BUILD THEIR HOMES?

Chapter 1

Most settlers in colonial America lived in wooden houses. In a town like Bayberry Cove, the houses were quite small with only two rooms—a kitchen, called the hall, for cooking, eating, and working; and a bed chamber where the whole family slept together. Later, they might add a third room, called the front hall, which was used only for special occasions. But first they had to build their homes. That took a lot of wood and a lot of work.

THE POWER TOOL

When the first European colonists arrived in North America, they brought with them a very powerful tool. It enabled them to build homes, forts, villages, bridges, and roads. The Native American tribes were so impressed by this tool, they willingly traded many useful things—including animal hides, birch bark canoes, and skillfully woven baskets—in order to obtain one.

Birch bark canoe

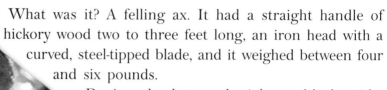

What was it? A felling ax. It had a straight handle of hickory wood two to three feet long, an iron head with a curved, steel-tipped blade, and it weighed between four and six pounds.

During the later colonial era, blacksmiths improved the design, making the head flatter and the blade sharper and shorter. This new ax gave tree fellers a steadier, more accurate swing. It worked so well, it is still made and used today. It was the first great American invention, and it changed the world.

Felling ax

THE TREE FELLERS

The first thing the colonists saw when they arrived in America was wood, and plenty of it. Forests dense with oak, maple, chestnut, holly, dogwood, black walnut, yellowwood, beech, birch, poplar, spruce, and pine trees stretched along the east coast of America from New England to the Carolinas.

While they cut enough wood to build permanent structures, the Europeans lived in temporary shelters they had dug into hillsides like caves. Why didn't they adapt the architecture of the people already living in America? Some did, building Native American–style longhouses with frames of supple branches and walls of birch bark or woven straw. Longhouses were warm, lightweight, and easy to move. They had served Native Americans well for hundreds of years and could have become the main form of housing for the colonists, too. But people from Europe wanted houses that looked like those back home. They wanted something that would make them feel "at home"—houses with solid walls, roofs, stone chimneys, shingles, shutters, and doors. That took a lot of wood—and a lot of work.

HOUSE RAISING

Fieldstone chimney

Before settlers could raise a house, they had to dig a foundation two to three feet deep and line it with stones

Longhouses were built by the Iroquois tribes of northeastern America. The Iroquois often called themselves the Haudenosaunee, which means People of the Longhouse.

and mortar. The mortar was made from crushed limestone or clay mixed with water. It kept the foundation watertight.

Next, they built a chimney of fieldstone. In New England, the chimney was built in the center of the foundation, where it could warm the entire house during the long, cold winters. In the southern colonies, where the weather was warmer, the chimney rose from one end of the house so that some of the heat would radiate outward.

Trees were cut during the winter, and the logs were stacked and left to season. During seasoning, moisture in the logs evaporated, leaving the wood dry and strong. The best quality wood for building was often seasoned for at least a year.

In addition to axes, colonial builders had a wide range of other tools. A tool with a blade like a curved hoe, called an adze, scraped the logs clean. Chisels and bow saws sliced the logs into boards. Chalk and string were the colonial "measuring tape," used to mark width and

A swinging arm called a crane was attached to the fireplace wall. Pots of water, soup, or cornmeal pudding could be swung over the fire for cooking, or over the hearth for serving.

length. Spike-shaped awls made holes for wooden pegs, and heavy mallets pounded the pegs in. Pulleys hoisted the beams that supported the roof.

The early colonists did not have glass windowpanes. Heavy shutters on either side of each window were used to close the windows at night and during the winter to keep the house warm. Sometimes people would scrape a piece of leather very thin, rub it with fat to make it almost transparent, and stretch it across the window to make a "pane." Real glass was not available to most colonists until the early eighteenth century, when greater prosperity enabled them to afford many new things.

A house-raising involved the entire community. While men constructed the house frame, women prepared meals over an open fire. Children ran errands and fetched water. Everyone did something. Helping another family build their house guaranteed they would help you build yours.

Little Shavers
Save the Day

When colonial builders wanted to join two pieces of lumber together, they couldn't just reach for a nail. Why? Iron nails were forged by hand and very difficult to obtain. What did they use instead? Wooden pegs, or trunnels.

Wooden pegs may not look very strong, but wood expands and contracts as the weather changes. After a few years, the pegs would form an extremely tight fit with the boards and hold as well as a metal nail.

Building a home could require hundreds of wooden pegs. Colonial boys often spent long winter evenings whittling pegs. Pegs had to be shaved to a fine point with a small knife, and a good whittler left many shavings behind.

Have you ever heard someone call little boys "little shavers"? Does this phrase go back to colonial days when boys shaved wooden pegs? No one knows for certain. We do know, however, that without these pegs, many colonial homes would have never been built, so we can easily say that when it came to construction, little shavers did indeed save the day.

Colonial cooks used plenty of equipment, including pots, kettles, saucepans, pot hooks, a wide, flat shovel to hold pies and bread, big spoons for stirring, and long, pointed pokers for tending the fire.

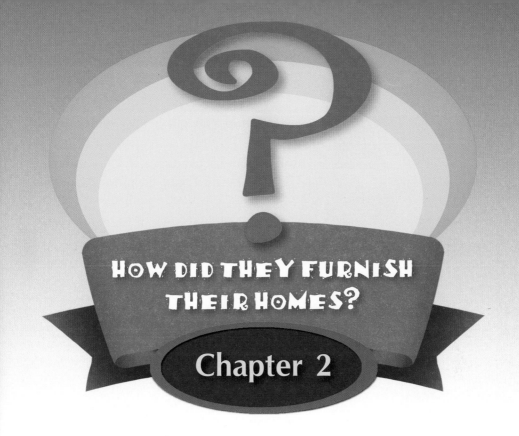

HOW DID THEY FURNISH THEIR HOMES?

Chapter 2

The average colonial family didn't have much furniture. In the kitchen they sat on stools or benches and ate off a long table called a trestle. The bedroom had one large bed and one or two smaller ones tucked underneath. Wealthy families might have elegantly carved cabinets and chests of drawers. Both rich and poor, though, gathered around the fireplace at night to say their evening prayers, share stories, and sing hymns and songs.

KEEPING THE HOME FIRES BURNING

The fireplace was the heart of the home, used for warmth, light, and cooking. The fire never went out. It was tended all day and banked at night with ashes that kept the embers warm. What happened if it did go out? Then a child was sent to a neighbor's house with a covered iron pan to collect a bit of smoldering wood and bring it back home. In rural areas, this could involve a round-trip of several miles.

During the eighteenth century, colonists began to use tinderboxes to start fires. A tinderbox was a small, metal box with holes in the top and a bit of charred cloth inside. Striking a piece of steel and a flint stone together above the holes would cause a spark to leap inside the

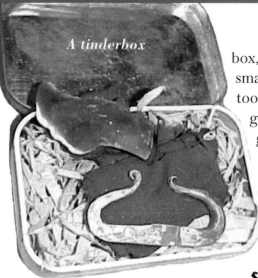

A tinderbox

box, igniting the cloth and generating a small fire. Lighting a fire with a tinderbox took skill and practice. If the tinderbox got too hot, it could do more harm than good.

In colonial days, if someone called you "a real tinderbox," it meant you had a hot temper and those around you should watch out!

MAKING YOUR BED AND SLEEPING IN IT, TOO

The most important piece of furniture in the colonial home was the bed. A good bed was built so high off the floor, people needed steps to climb onto it. Why so high? Underneath was a smaller bed that could be pulled or "trundled" out at night and pushed back during the day. Children slept together in the trundle beds, and the grown-ups

Most quilts in colonial days were very plain, but sometimes women would add colorful embroidery or needlework, which made the quilt a prized possession to their children and grandchildren.

in the main bed. Households usually had far more people than beds. Unless your family was very wealthy, chances are you would never have a bed to yourself while you were growing up.

How would you make your bed? With straw and feathers. Mattresses consisted of straw stuffed into linen or wool coverlets. Stuffing mattresses was a job for the summer, when straw was fresh. The mattresses had to last an entire year. By the end of the winter, the straw was usually damp and smelly. Everyone looked forward to a freshly stuffed

The coverlet for a straw mattress was called a "straw tick" or tycke. Today, the striped canvas used to cover many mattresses is called ticking.

mattress, even if the new straw felt prickly and poked you through the coverlet.

For blankets, colonists used quilts called feather beds. Whenever a bird was plucked for cooking, the cook would make sure to save the down—the soft, light feathers closest to a bird's skin. It takes a lot of down to fill a quilt. Children spent many hours cleaning and sorting the feathers and stuffing the feather beds. The chore might have been

Cabinetmakers needed knives and chisels of many different sizes to carve decorative patterns in the wood. A turning lathe was also used to create curved surfaces and rounded edges.

boring, but it was also very rewarding when you finally got to snuggle under a nice warm quilt on a cold winter night.

What other furniture did the colonists have? Benches, three-legged stools, and plain, pine board tables were used in the kitchens. Oak chests provided storage for clothes and valuable items. Some chests had small compartments that could be drawn in and out, making them the original "chest of drawers."

What about closets? Colonial homes didn't have the built-in closets we use today. Closets were tall freestanding cabinets called wardrobes—or armoires, if you preferred French.

Skilled furniture makers were called cabinetmakers, and they were among the most valued craftsmen in the colonies. Even the Puritans, who looked down upon fancy decorations, appreciated well-made furniture. Colonial cabinetmakers produced many beautiful pieces, some of which survive in museums.

FYInfo

John Winthrop's Fork

At mealtimes, colonial children set the table with wooden bowls called trenchers, pewter mugs, wooden spoons, and one or two knives that could be shared among several people. What about forks? Nobody used them.

In 1630, John Winthrop imported the first fork to America. Winthrop served as governor of the Massachusetts Bay Colony for several terms. He is most famous for a sermon he gave calling upon the Puritans to make their colony an example all people could look up to, like "a city upon a hill." Obviously, Winthrop was a very important person.

But what happened to his fork? Did he ever eat with it? Probably not. Table forks weren't used until the early nineteenth century.

The first forks looked quite strange to most people. Many clergymen condemned them as sinful. God meant people to eat with their fingers, not metal prongs, they declared. Forks were also more difficult to make than spoons, so perhaps that is another reason people continued to use their fingers.

In a Puritan home, it was perfectly polite to eat your meal with your fingers and wipe them on the edges of your sleeves. Sleeves were often made especially long just for this purpose. Talking at the table, though, was considered rude. After saying grace together, everyone ate in silence, the only sounds coming from the clatter of knives and spoons, but never, of course, forks.

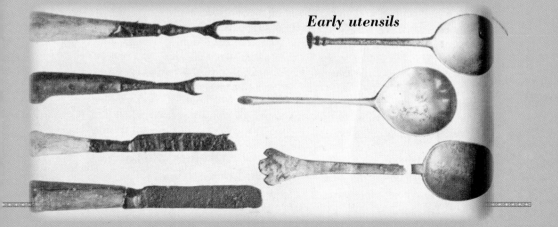

Early utensils

An Iroquois longhouse could be large enough for two or more families. Raised platforms along the sides were covered with fur hides and used for both sleeping and sitting. Everyone shared the fire in the center.

HOW DID THEY EAT?

Chapter 3

Most Europeans came to America from cities, not farms. Back home, they had bought their meat from butcher shops, their bread from bakeries, and their vegetables from market stalls. They had no experience living off the land, and if they didn't learn fast, they did not survive.

Fortunately, the colonists found help. In Jamestown, they became friends with the Powhatan tribe. In New England, the Wampanoags, under the leadership of Chief Massasoit, came to the aid of the Puritans. In the mid-Atlantic region, the tribes of the Iroquois Federation assisted Dutch and German settlers.

THE THREE SISTERS

Each of the native tribes had its own traditions. They all, however, knew the Three Sisters.

Who were these sisters? Corn (or maize), squash, and beans—the three great crops of the Americas. Cornmeal pudding, pumpkin stew, and baked beans became the everyday fare of the colonists and kept them from starving as they built their new homes.

CORN

BEANS

SQUASH

Each plant helped the others grow. The corn stalk supported the climbing beans. The beans enriched the soil with nitrogen, and the large leaves of the squash prevented weeds from taking root.

Native Americans planted the three crops all together in a circular pattern, rather than in separate rows—a method the colonists imitated. A dead fish planted at the foot of each cornstalk enriched the soil. The garden may have smelled a little fishy afterward, but it had plenty of natural fertilizer!

Native Americans also introduced Europeans to cranberries, blueberries, beach plums, wild grapes, and other fruits. Nut-bearing trees were an excellent source of food, too, especially the American chestnut tree. Wild chestnuts had a sweet carrotlike flavor, and gathering chestnuts was something children looked forward to every fall.

HUNTING AND FISHING

Wild game in North America was so plentiful, Native Americans did not have to breed domesticated animals for food. The colonists quickly learned how to hunt for deer, squirrels, rabbits, muskrats, quail, ducks, partridges, pigeons, and many other mammals and birds.

The coastal waters were abundant with fish. Like Native Americans, colonists preferred to fish with nets instead of baited hooks. New England became known as the "land of the cod" after the enormous schools of Atlantic codfish that swam along the shore. Digging for clams and catching crabs kept children busy during warm weather. Lobsters were easy to find and catch, but early colonists were not familiar with them and often used them for fertilizer rather than food. Only much later did lobster become the delicacy we consider it today.

The fibers of plants such as flax, cattails, milkweed, and Indian hemp, also called dogbane, could all be twisted into long, sturdy cords to make fishing nets.

Meat and fish were both preserved by smoking, a process of drying meat by hanging it over a smoldering fire for several weeks or even months. In the south, hickory was a favorite smoking wood. The label "Hickory Smoked" still stands for flavor today, even if the hickory comes from artificial chemicals instead of a tree!

GRAZING ON THE COMMON

Ever hear of Boston Common? (If you think this book has left out the *the* before *Common*, you're wrong. True Bostonians just call it Boston

Common.) Today it is a big urban park, but in colonial America the town common was a pasture where everyone brought their cows to graze. How could you be sure which animal was yours? Mark its ear! Owners clipped their cows' ears with a particular design or pattern. Today, *earmark* means "to set something aside for a special use," and the term goes back to colonial days when each family earmarked their cows for their own use.

Butter churn

Without refrigeration to keep it fresh, most milk was allowed to sour or "clabber" to make sour cream or cheese. Every household had a butter churn, which even small children knew how to use. You can make butter yourself by shaking heavy cream in a jar or churning it with a wire whisk. The liquid left behind is called buttermilk. The taste of buttermilk has a slight tang.

Colonists liked to use buttermilk in the cornmeal pancakes they called johnnycakes. Why *Johnny*? Some historians think these quickly made cakes were originally called "journey cakes" because they were easy to roll up and take on a journey. If you were a colonial child setting off on an errand on a winter day, a hot journey cake could keep your hands warm, too—that is, if you didn't eat it right away.

DUTCH TREATS

One of the most important Dutch contributions to colonial cooking was the Dutch oven, a deep, three-legged cast-iron pot with a close-fitting lid and long handle. Dutch ovens were used for everything from stews to puddings. They were always welcome at a house-raising, where food needed to be kept hot and cooks fed dozens of hungry workers several times a day.

Another Dutch contribution is one every American young or old can name—the cookie. *Koekje* means "little cake" in Dutch. In 1796, Amelia Simmons published *American Cookery*, the first American cookbook. She included two recipes for little Dutch cakes, spelling the word c-o-o-k-i-e, and Americans have been happily eating cookies ever since.

Corn Pudding: An Everyday Colonial Dish

If you grew up in colonial America, you would have eaten cornmeal every day. It didn't matter if you were English, Dutch, German, French, African, or Native American. Everyone ate corn.

Dried corn was ground with stones, and the resulting meal was boiled or baked. Amelia Simmons included three recipes for "Indian pudding" in her book, *American Cookery* (1796). Cornmeal pudding was also called hasty pudding, though there was nothing hasty about her recipes. One of them called for the pudding to be boiled for twelve hours! Simmons did not give exact measurements for many ingredients, which makes her recipes hard to follow. Here's a modern adaptation of one you can try:

Cornmeal Pudding
3 cups milk
$1/2$ cup molasses
$1/3$ cup yellow cornmeal
$1/2$ teaspoon ginger
$1/2$ teaspoon ground
    cinnamon
$1/4$ teaspoon salt
1 tablespoon butter

In a saucepan, mix milk and molasses; stir in cornmeal, ginger, cinnamon, and salt. Cook and stir until thick, about 10 minutes. Stir in butter. Turn into a 1-quart casserole. Bake uncovered at 300° Fahrenheit for about 1 hour. Serves 6.

A woman uses a foot peddle, or treadle, to turn her wheel. Some models required the user to stand and turn the wheel by hand, a far more tiring way to spin.

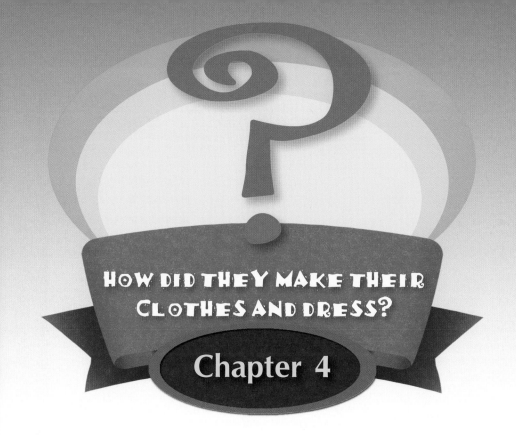

HOW DID THEY MAKE THEIR CLOTHES AND DRESS?

Chapter 4

Although many fabrics could be imported from Europe, most colonists could not afford to pay high prices for cloth. Instead, they spun wool from their own sheep and made linen from flax. They also learned how to dye their fabrics cranberry red, mulberry blue, butternut brown, pine green, and other vibrant colors using the native plants of their new land.

THE DISTAFF SIDE

Sheep were sheared every spring. The wool was then washed and carded with a stiff brush that forced all the fibers to flow in one direction, making it easier to spin the wool into thread.

From the time she learned how to walk, nearly every colonial girl took her distaff and spindle with her wherever she went. The distaff was a long stick, forked at the upper end, upon which she bound a thick bunch of carded wool. The spindle was a shorter stick, sharpened to a point at one end, with a clay or stone knob, called a whorl, at the other.

The spinning girl carried her distaff under one arm and used her opposite hand to pull out a few strands of wool and twist them into

A spindle (left) and a cherry wood distaff. The distaff was carved in 1998 by Mera Matthews of Smith College as part of an exhibit on women and the history of technology.

a thread. As the thread grew longer, she would wind it around the pointed end of the spindle by rotating the whorl.

The distaff and spindle could also be attached to a spinning wheel. Like a lullaby, the constant hum of the spinning wheel must have put many children to sleep at night, for the spinning wheel was as essential to the colonial home as the hearth. Women and girls spent so much time spinning that people began to refer to the mother's side of the family as the "distaff side," a phrase still used today.

THREAD INTO CLOTH

Some women wove cloth at home on a square loom. The result was a rough, sturdy fabric known as homespun. In larger villages, women could sell their thread to professional weavers who made a finer, smoother cloth for the wealthier families.

Though we think of colonial Americans as dressed in sober gray and black, many of them liked clothes of rich colors. Dyes were made

from a wide range of plants. Cranberries created a deep red; grapes, a dark purple. Onion skins produced a pale yellow shade; walnuts, a deep brown; and the outer skins of pumpkins and squash, bright orange. Dyes were fixed on the cloth using a solution of hot water and vinegar—much the way people set the dye on Easter eggs today.

In addition to wool, colonists also wove linen, a light cottonlike fabric made from flax, a tall grass with a fibrous stem. After it was harvested, the flax was soaked for several days and then beaten with wooden mallets to separate the fibers from the stem. Spinning flax was more difficult than spinning wool. A girl who was a skillful flax spinner could count on a steady income and made a very desirable wife!

PUDDING CAPS AND PETTICOATS

In 1670, a wealthy Boston merchant, Robert Gibbs, hired an artist to paint portraits of his three children—Margaret, aged seven; Robert junior, aged four; and baby Henry, only eighteen months old. Like children today, they wore their best clothes for their pictures.

Little Henry looked quite dignified in a long dress with big, puffy sleeves, a long apron, and a pudding on his head. No, he wasn't wearing a bowl full of dessert. A pudding was a padded cap intended to protect a baby's head if he fell. Though we can't see behind him, Henry probably had long strings attached to the back of his apron at his shoulders. Like reins, these "leads" could be held by his mother or older siblings to keep him from wandering off or getting too close to the fire.

Both boys and girls wore long dresses until the age of five or six. After that they dressed like adults. A boy was said to be "breeched" when he got his first pair of pants.

What would his breeches look like? The same artist also painted a group portrait of the three children of John Mason, a successful baker. For his portrait, eight-year-old David wore a pair of short trousers. The edges of his under drawers, called "small clothes," hung below the breeches and were gathered at his knees. His close-fitting jacket, or "doublet," sported slashes in the sleeves to display his white linen shirt. In one hand he carried a pair of gloves, and in the other a walking stick—like a true colonial gentleman.

What did girls wear? Like David Mason, seven-year-old Margaret Gibbs appears very grown-up in her portrait. She wore a long dress with a stiff bib, called a stomacher, shaped like a V to give her a narrow waist. Beneath her dress, she wore a simple white sleeveless garment called a shift. Around her shift she wore a pair of stays, a lace-up corset reinforced with willow rods or whalebone, to give her good posture. Over the stays, she put on two or three petticoats, and over those an underskirt, overskirt, blouse, vest, and apron. She didn't wear under drawers, though, for it was considered highly improper for women to wear pants of any kind.

Stomacher

Both boys and girls wore stockings knitted from wool and held up by ribbon garters. Their shoes were square-toed with heavy buckles. Cobblers did not distinguish between left and right, so both shoes were shaped alike and could be worn on either foot.

The children in these paintings were far wealthier than most colonial children, but they do show us some general truths. In colonial America, childhood was considered a serious time. By dressing as adults, children learned how to behave as adults and assume their responsibilities in their families and the larger community.

Colonial shoe

Moccasins: The Original American Shoe

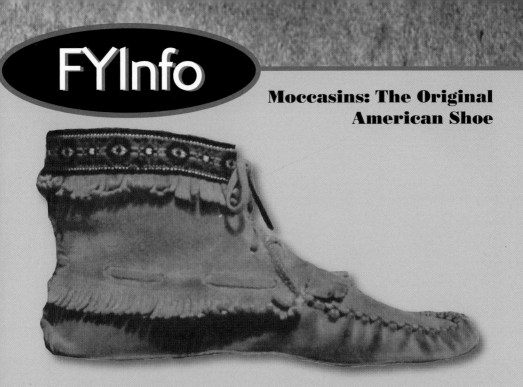

European Americans may have liked their traditional clothing, but when they went hunting, they followed in the footsteps of the Native Americans—literally.

The word *moccasin* comes from Algonquian. Every tribe had its own distinct style of moccasin, and Native Americans could often tell what tribe someone belonged to by their footwear. Europeans generally weren't aware of this, but they did know that moccasins enabled them to move silently through the woods.

In Virginia, a story is still told about a group of young men who lived in the backwoods and decided they preferred to dress entirely as Native Americans year round. When they appeared in church in their native dress one summer Sunday, they caused quite a stir—for Europeans spent the summer buttoned up in linen and wool, while Native Americans wore very little at all. What happened? No one knows for sure. Most likely, they were sent away and told not to come back until they were "properly" attired in breeches and waistcoats.

Nevertheless, Native American garments continued to be favored by frontiersmen for the next two hundred years. Today, moccasins keep millions of feet comfortable at work, at play, or at school.

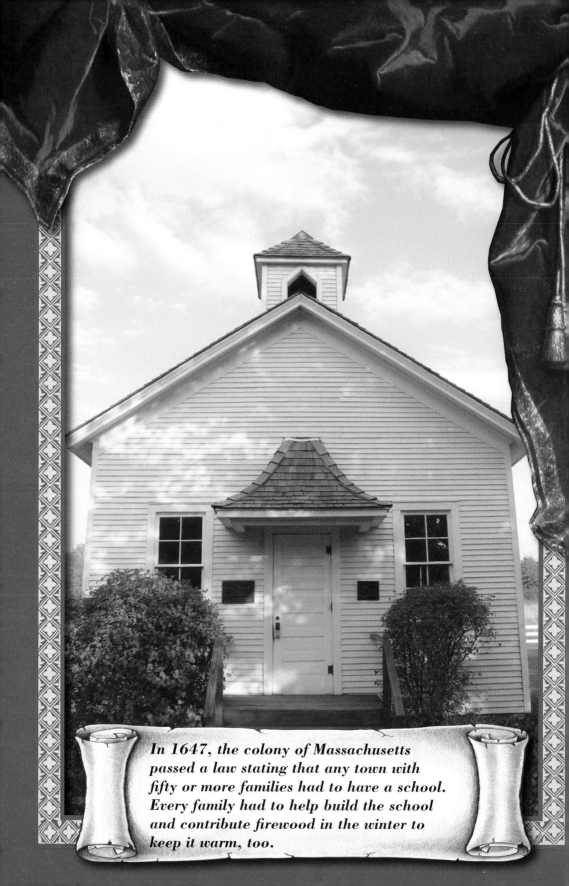

In 1647, the colony of Massachusetts passed a law stating that any town with fifty or more families had to have a school. Every family had to help build the school and contribute firewood in the winter to keep it warm, too.

HOW WERE THEY EDUCATED?

Chapter 5

Colonial people of all social classes valued education. Wealthy families could hire private tutors for their sons and sometimes for their daughters too. Many towns and villages maintained a dame school for little children and a grammar school for older boys. Older girls usually stayed home to learn the skills necessary for running a household. Reading and writing were important, however, and everyone tried to learn their ABCs.

First published in Boston in 1690, *The New England Primer* became one of America's most popular schoolbooks. It remained in print until the early twentieth century. Generations of children knew each verse by heart.

Some rhymes were pleasant:
> *The **N**ightingales sing*
> *In time of spring*

Others, harsh:
> *The idle **F**ool*
> *Is whipt at school*

The Colonial ABCs

In Adam's Fall
We sinned all.
Thy Life to Mend
*This **B**ook Attend.*
*The **C**at doth play*
And after slay.
> *—The New England*
> *Primer*

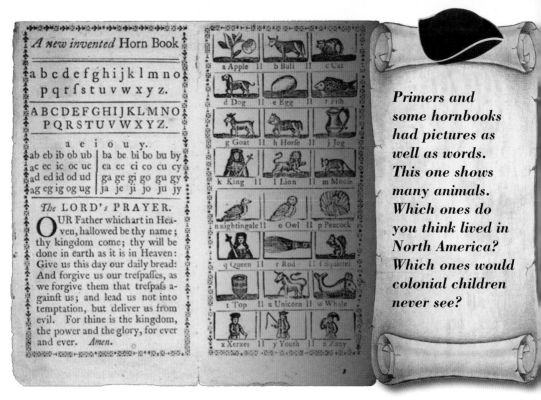

A *new invented* Horn Book

a b c d e f g h i j k l m n o
p q r ſ s t u v w x y z.

A B C D E F G H I J K L M N O
P Q R S T U V W X Y Z.

a e i o u y.

ab eb ib ob ub | ba be bi bo bu by
ac ec ic oc uc | ca ce ci co cu cy
ad ed id od ud | ga ge gi go gu gy
ag eg ig og ug | ja je ji jo ju jy

The LORD'ſ PRAYER.

OUR Father whichart in Heaven, hallowed be thy name;
thy kingdom come; thy will be
done in earth as it is in Heaven:
Give us this day our daily bread:
And forgive us our treſpaſſes, as
we forgive them that treſpaſs a-
gainſt us; and lead us not into
temptation, but deliver us from
evil. For thine is the kingdom,
the power and the glory, for ever
and ever. *Amen.*

a Apple | b Bull | c Cat
d Dog | e Egg | f Fiſh
g Goat | h Horſe | j Jug
k King | l Lion | m Mouſe
n nightingale | o Owl | p Peacock
q Queen | r Rod | ſ Squirrel
t Top | u Unicorn | w Whale
x Xerxes | y Youth | z Zany

Primers and some hornbooks had pictures as well as words. This one shows many animals. Which ones do you think lived in North America? Which ones would colonial children never see?

Were colonial children whipped at school? Yes, but not for talking. They were more likely to be whipped for being quiet. The colonial schoolhouse consisted of a single room where children of all ages crowded onto long benches. The schoolmaster stood at the front and expected to hear the students reading or reciting their lessons out loud continuously. How else could he be sure they were learning? Everybody spoke at once. The schoolroom was a buzzing hive of different voices. A silent student was considered a lazy student—or worse yet, a day-dreamer. The teacher would call the unfortunate culprit to the front, and the birch rod would come down until he or she started speaking, loud and clear again.

HORNBOOKS

Before children could read the primer, they learned their letters from a hornbook. A hornbook was a square wooden paddle with a sheet of paper on which the alphabet had been written attached to one side and covered with a smooth piece horn. (Cattle horns consist of the

same material as fingernails. When soaked they become soft, and layers of horn can be peeled off and flattened.) Some hornbooks also had a prayer or short verse from the Bible. Often, a string was passed through a hole in the handle so that children could hang their hornbooks around their neck and keep them handy. As children outgrew their hornbooks, they would pass them on to younger siblings or cousins. This probably explains why so few are left today. If you do happen to see one in a museum, it will look very well used indeed.

WRITING

Quill and ink

When it came to writing, colonial children were still back in the "stone age"! Because paper was scarce, most of them learned to write on a shard of stone slate, using a piece of limestone or charcoal for chalk.

If a family could afford paper, children would be able to practice their penmanship with quills and ink. Quill pens were made from goose or wild turkey feathers filed to a sharp point. Ink was concocted by boiling oak, cherry, or chestnut bark with a little vinegar and salt. Students displayed good penmanship with pride, for it was considered the mark of a truly educated person.

LEARNING THROUGH APPRENTICESHIP

Education involved more than reading and writing. Most children were also expected to learn a skilled trade or craft. Some were taught by their parents; others became apprentices to professional craftsmen. An apprenticeship usually began when a child was between the ages of ten and twelve and lasted up to seven years. During that time the apprentice had to live in the employer's household and was expected to be obedient and helpful at all times.

A boy could be an apprentice to a blacksmith, silversmith, barrel maker or cooper, papermaker, printer, bookbinder, glass blower, cabinetmaker, wheelwright, shipwright, bricklayer, carpenter, gunsmith, or saddler.

The most important accomplishments for girls were cooking and spinning, but many girls learned a trade too. Among trades open to girls were hat maker or milliner, dressmaker, candle maker or chandler, candy maker, wigmaker, and hairdresser.

If you were a hairdresser, you would have had a lot of real dummies for clients! Why? Colonial hairdressers styled hair on wigs, not people. Customers would drop off their hair at the shop on a wooden head, or "dummy," and pick it up after it had been styled and powdered white. Hairdressers were in high demand in towns like New Amsterdam and Williamsburg, Virginia, where both men and women wore elaborate wigs and liked to keep up with the latest fashions from Europe.

WAS EDUCATION FOR EVERYONE?

African Americans faced many barriers to education. Slaves had limited opportunities to learn how to read and write. In the southern colonies, laws forbade them to do so. Even where they were free, they often found themselves unwelcome in colonial schools. Many African Americans persisted in their pursuit of education, though, and by the middle of the eighteenth century, African Americans could be found in a wide range of trades and professions.

Native Americans had less interest in Anglo-European schools because their own culture was still intact. In 1711, Governor Alexander Spotswood of Virginia founded a school for Native American boys, but it did not impress the local chiefs.

Why should their sons learn how to be like Englishmen, the chiefs asked, when Englishmen did not think their own children should become like Native Americans? Some Native Americans did learn how to read and write from Christian missionaries, and these skills no doubt helped them serve as liaisons between the two cultures.

Education in colonial America meant different things to different peoples. All of them agreed, however, that it was important for children to learn the skills that would help their communities grow and thrive.

Poor Richard's Almanack: America's First Bestseller

In 1732, a little book called *Poor Richard's Almanack* appeared on the shelves of Philadelphia booksellers. It was filled with short, witty, wise, and clever sayings that gave advice on just about every subject. Richard published a new almanac each year until 1758. By then he was a best-selling author with thousands of loyal readers throughout the colonies. Who was he? None other than Benjamin Franklin—colonial America's most famous scientist, inventor, social reformer, and philosopher.

Poor Richard's Almanack is still in print. Here are a few of the most well known sayings, also called aphorisms:

> Poor Richard, 1733.
>
> AN
>
> # Almanack
>
> For the Year of Chrift
>
> # 1733,
>
> Being the Firft after LEAP YEAR:
>
> | And makes fince the Creation | Years |
> |---|---|
> | By the Account of the Eaftern *Greeks* | 7241 |
> | By the Latin Church, when ☉ ent, ♈ | 6932 |
> | By the Computation of *W.W.* | 5742 |
> | By the *Roman* Chronology | 5682 |
> | By the *Jewifh* Rabbies | 5494 |
>
> *Wherein is contained*
> The Lunations, Eclipfes, Judgment of the Weather, Spring Tides, Planets Motions & mutual Afpects, Sun and Moon's Rifing and Setting, Length of Days, Time of High Water, Fairs, Courts, and obfervable Days.
> Fitted to the Latitude of Forty Degrees, and a Meridian of Five Hours Weft from *London*, but may without fenfible Error, ferve all the adjacent Places, even from *Newfoundland* to *South-Carolina.*
>
> By *RICHARD SAUNDERS*, Philom.
>
> PHILADELPHIA:
> Printed and fold by *B. FRANKLIN*, at the New Printing-Office near the Market.

- There are no gains without pains.
- Have you something to do tomorrow? Do it today.
- If you would be wealthy, think of saving as well as getting.
- Love your neighbor, yet don't pull down your hedge.
- The rotten apple spoils his companions.

Are any of these familiar to you? Can you rephrase them in your own words? Do you think they are as true today as they were in Franklin's time?

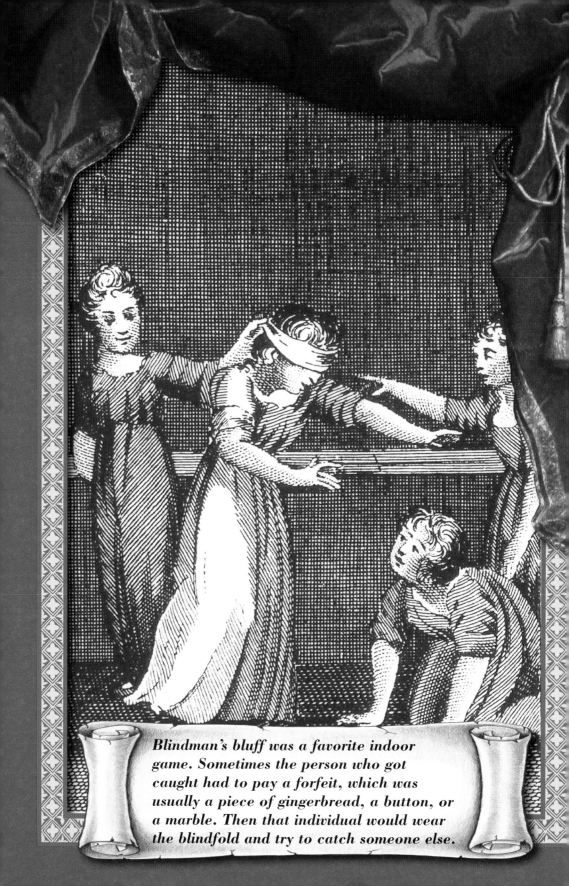

Blindman's bluff was a favorite indoor game. Sometimes the person who got caught had to pay a forfeit, which was usually a piece of gingerbread, a button, or a marble. Then that individual would wear the blindfold and try to catch someone else.

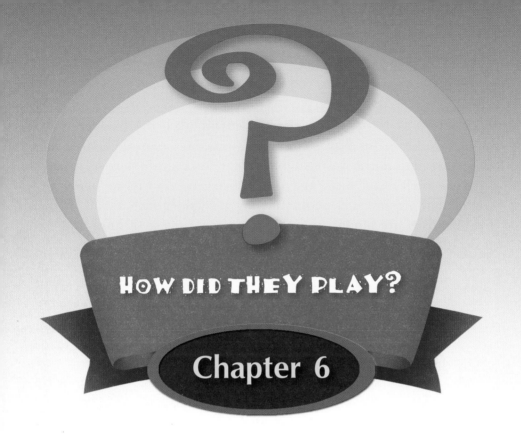

HOW DID THEY PLAY?

Chapter 6

Was life really all work and no play for colonial children? No. Even with all their chores and responsibilities, they were still children, and they still found time to play. Because most homes were small and crowded, children found their best play spaces outside. Have you ever played hide-and-seek, tag, tug-of-war, or leapfrog? Colonial children played those games too. They also played blindman's bluff, king of the hill, jump rope, jacks, marbles, ninepins, and quoits, a variation of ring toss. In winter, children and adults would ice-skate on skates with blades of sharpened cattle bones. They would coast down snowy hills on wooden to-boggans. (The word *toboggan* comes from the native Micmac people of Canada.)

What about ball games? Colonial children played catch, but not with a rubber ball. They used an inflated pig's bladder instead. The membranes of the bladder are strong and elastic, and an empty bladder could be blown up like a balloon. A small

Colonial prairie doll

duct serves as the air tube and is tied off once the bladder is firm enough to toss. This may seem yucky to us, but colonial children knew that when an animal was slaughtered for food, every part of it had to be used—bone, hair, hide, and internal organs, as well as meat. They found nothing unusual about turning a bladder into a ball. In fact, bladder balls are among the oldest playing balls in history and have been used in many cultures around the world.

TOYS THAT GREW ON TREES

Cup and ball

Most colonial children did not have store-bought toys, but they did find toys growing on trees. Girls fashioned dolls with apples for heads, sticks for bodies, and leaves for dresses. Acorn caps made miniature teacups, and walnut halves, bowls. A toy boat could be made from a piece of bark with a leaf for a sail.

Almost anything in nature could become a toy. Flat stones were good for skipping across ponds, a game that took a steady hand and a lot of skill. Flowers with long stems could be woven into necklaces, chains, and bracelets.

Small scraps of wood offered endless possibilities. An expert whittler could produce a steady supply of spinning tops, toy animals, and building blocks for the amusement of little children and older ones, too.

Fife

MUSIC, SONG, AND DANCE

Colonial children went to a lot of parties—quilting parties, corn shucking parties, apple cider pressing parties, and house-raising parties. Any time three or more people gathered together to work, they could make a party.

Working parties provided ample opportunity to tell riddles, share stories, and sing rounds. Certainly, music made any job go faster. In every crowd,

someone was bound to have a fiddle or a fife, and after the work was done, the dancing could begin.

People danced in a large group, rather than as separate couples. The adults formed a big circle or two long lines. The children stood on the outside, watching and learning the steps by following along. Scottish reels, French gavottes, and English contra dances were all favorites. Dancers changed partners as they moved around the circle or down the line. The trick was to get back to your original partner before the music stopped!

Children in 1939 learning a colonial dance. Groups in costume still perform at historic sites, where they teach visitors about early American history.

TAKING A HOLIDAY

In 1621, the Pilgrims of Plymouth gathered together to celebrate a successful harvest after a long and difficult year. This became known as the first Thanksgiving. Today, Thanksgiving is celebrated on the third Thursday of November. In colonial America, however, Thanksgiving was not a formal holiday, but any day people agreed to set aside

Sinterklaas

to give thanks. It was often observed more by prayer and fasting than by feasting.

Though Puritan ministers in Massachusetts discouraged any celebration of Christmas, English colonists in Virginia welcomed it with dancing and music. Dutch children in New Amsterdam set their shoes out on the eve of December 6 for St. Nicholas, or Sinterklaas. They woke up the next morning to find them filled with gingerbread if they had been good or thorns if they hadn't.

May 1, or May Day, was an old English holiday celebrated in the southern and mid-Atlantic colonies by dancing around a May pole decorated with flowers and ribbons. April 1, of course, was Fool's Day, a time for riddles and practical jokes. All Hallow's Eve was observed by Scottish settlers on the last day of October. They lit candles and banged on drums to chase away any ghosts that might be lingering nearby.

The favorite holiday of most colonial children, however, had no special name. It was simply called market day or fair day. Once or twice a year, people would assemble on the village common to trade livestock and other kinds of goods, from beaver skins and deer hide to cheddar cheese and mince pies. Few people had money, so everyone came with something to barter, and everyone tried to go home with a bargain.

While the trading went on, the local militia drilled on the fairgrounds. Sometimes traveling jugglers and puppeteers put on shows, too. Races, wrestling, and target shooting contests with bows and arrows attracted eager participants and spectators. Musicians played far into the night. Both children and adults agreed that a fair was the best way of turning work into play.

A New American Instrument

Africans introduced many new musical instruments to the colonies, including beaded rattles, several different kinds of drums, and a stringed instrument made out of a long-necked gourd sliced in half, with strands of horsehair stretched across the scooped-out hollow. This instrument was called a *mbanza* in Kimbundu, a language spoken in northwest and central Africa.

In America, *mbanza* players added more strings to their instrument and changed the design to make it more like the European guitar. After a while, the word *mbanza* became *banzo* and then *banjo*, an instrument with a truly American sound, played by bluegrass, folk, and jazz musicians to this day.

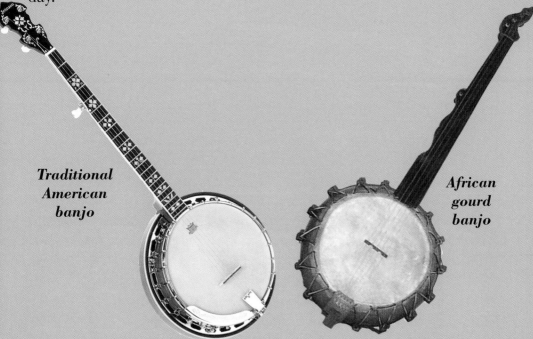

Traditional American banjo

African gourd banjo

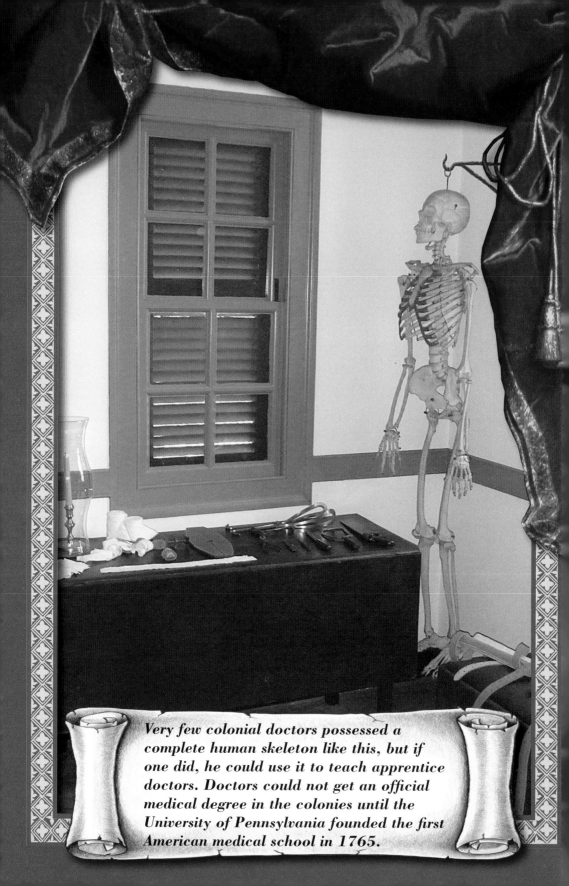

Very few colonial doctors possessed a complete human skeleton like this, but if one did, he could use it to teach apprentice doctors. Doctors could not get an official medical degree in the colonies until the University of Pennsylvania founded the first American medical school in 1765.

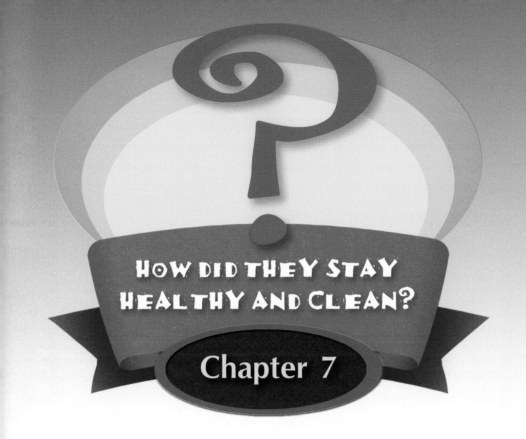

Illness was common in colonial America. People suffered from deadly diseases such as typhus, cholera, pneumonia, yellow fever, and smallpox. Many children died in their first years. Doctors knew nothing about germs and bacteria and often relied on superstition rather than science. Still, people tried to find the right cure for sickness. Sometimes they were lucky and actually succeeded!

GROWING YOUR OWN MEDICINE

In colonial America, every household had an herb garden that provided medicine as well as food. Mint, chives, rosemary, chamomile, lavender, thyme, yarrow, sage, and dill were all used in cures. Though many herbal remedies were chosen as a result of superstition, others have been found to have some solid biological basis. Garlic has small amounts of sulfur, an antibiotic. A solution of rosemary is mildly antiseptic (germ-killing) and can soothe bug bites and small wounds.

Native Americans shared many of their own plant-based medicines with the colonists. A tea made from pine needles could ward off scurvy during winter when other sources of vitamin C were scarce. Birch leaves, a traditional pain reliever, contain salicylate, the active ingredient in aspirin. The sassafras tree had so many uses it was called "nature's medicine chest." In the southern colonies, people made a tonic by steeping sassafras roots in boiling water with molasses. When this mixture fermented, they had the very first "root beer"!

CREEPY CURE WITH LEECHES

The apothecary shop served as the colonial drugstore. A successful apothecary stocked his shelves with imported spices, dried ginseng roots, bottled rum, oils made from plant extracts, and jars of hungry leeches.

Why leeches? In colonial days, doctors believed that diseases were caused by "bad humors." That doesn't mean they thought patients were grouches. "Humors" were the mysterious fluids in the body that supposedly kept the body in balance. Bleeding patients by applying leeches was one way to get rid of the bad humors.

Fortunately, most doctors prescribed only one, two, or three leeches at a time, and in most cases they couldn't suck out enough blood to

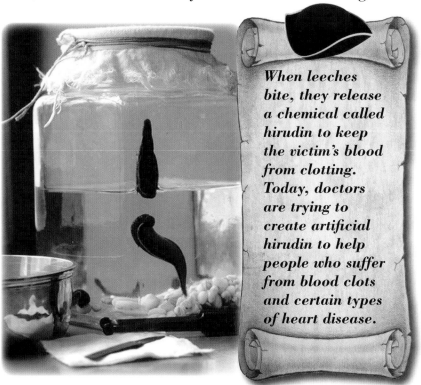

When leeches bite, they release a chemical called hirudin to keep the victim's blood from clotting. Today, doctors are trying to create artificial hirudin to help people who suffer from blood clots and certain types of heart disease.

do any serious harm. Best of all, when the leeching was done, the leech could be resold to the apothecary for the same fee at which it had been bought, a "money-back" guarantee.

INOCULATION: A MEDICAL BREAKTHROUGH

Smallpox was the most dreaded disease in colonial America. Nearly half of all its victims died. Those who survived were often scarred for life. There was no prevention and no cure. The only positive thing doctors knew about smallpox was that a person could not get it twice.

In 1706, a Massachusetts clergyman, Cotton Mather, learned about a process called inoculation from his African-born slave, Onesimus. Onesimus told Mather that when he was a child, he had been deliberately infected with smallpox through a small scratch on his shoulder, a common practice among his people in Africa. Afterward, he had come down with a very mild case of the disease, but was then protected for the rest of his life.

When a smallpox epidemic threatened Boston in 1721, Mather convinced Dr. Zabdiel Boylston to try inoculation. Boylston inoculated his own son and two others: his African American slave, Jack, and Jack's small son, Jackey. All three recovered completely.

Many Bostonians found the idea of inoculation unnatural and frightening. Boylston was threatened by riots and almost jailed. Undaunted, he continued to inoculate patients, and eventually inoculation became accepted throughout the colonies.

Unlike modern vaccination, inoculation did not completely eliminate smallpox. It did, however, reduce the number of deaths and establish the first step toward conquering the disease.

WHEN TAKING A BATH WAS AGAINST THE LAW

The Puritans may have believed "cleanliness is next to Godliness," but that doesn't mean they practiced what they preached. Colonial homes had no indoor plumbing. Water was brought in from wells, ponds, or streams. People filled small basins and washed only their face and hands.

Being completely naked, even if you were alone, was considered immodest, especially for women. When New England women did bathe, they kept their underskirts on. For a brief time, Philadelphia actually had a law forbidding anyone from bathing more than once a month—though it is not clear how city officials managed to enforce it.

Not all people opposed bathing. Native Americans built sweat lodges where they soaked in steam generated by pouring water over hot rocks. Dutch settlers enjoyed swimming in the natural hot springs of Saratoga in upstate New York. They claimed the springs were very beneficial to health, and Saratoga became so popular that by the 1760s even the English sought the "water cures" there.

What about toilets? In the country, it wasn't much of a problem. People simply "did their business" outdoors. In cities and towns, they used chamber pots and dumped the contents in back alleys and side streets. By our standards, colonial cities smelled terrible, but the inhabitants were used to it and hardly noticed.

Some families constructed outhouses in their backyards. These were seen as very modern conveniences. People who couldn't afford to build their own outhouses might rent one from their neighbors. Corncobs were the handiest form of toilet paper until the colonists finally manufactured enough newsprint to afford the luxury of being able to throw some away.

Thomas Jefferson invented one of America's first indoor toilets for his home, Monticello. It used a system of pulleys to empty the chamber pot through a hole in the floor into an underground "earth closet"—yet another ingenious accomplishment by the author of the Declaration of Independence!

Colonial outhouse

Just Add Water

What did the colonists use to wash themselves? A mixture of lye, fat, and salt. If that doesn't sound very effective, consider this: You use the same thing. It's called soap.

Lye is a liquid solution made by pouring water over wood ashes. It is highly caustic, which means it burns if you touch or taste it. When combined with the right amount of fat, though, a process called saponification takes place. During saponification, the lye and fat molecules join together to make a single long molecule with a "hook" at each end. In terms of chemistry, the molecule looks like this:

$$CH_3\text{-}(CH_2)_n\text{-}CO_2\text{-} +Na$$

When you wash with soap, one end of this molecule latches on to a microscopic piece of grime, the other attaches itself to a water molecule like a tiny chain, and, *whoosh*, the dirt is pulled right off.

Adding salt to the fat and lye mixture makes the liquid solidify, which is how soap cakes or bars are made.

The colonists made soap at home over an open fire. They didn't know the chemistry behind it, but they knew it helped them stay clean.

Making Soap
Step 1: Open cans of lye[*]
Step 2: Add lye
Step 3: Add fat
Step 4: Cook over fire

*The colonists had to make their lye. It was not available in cans.

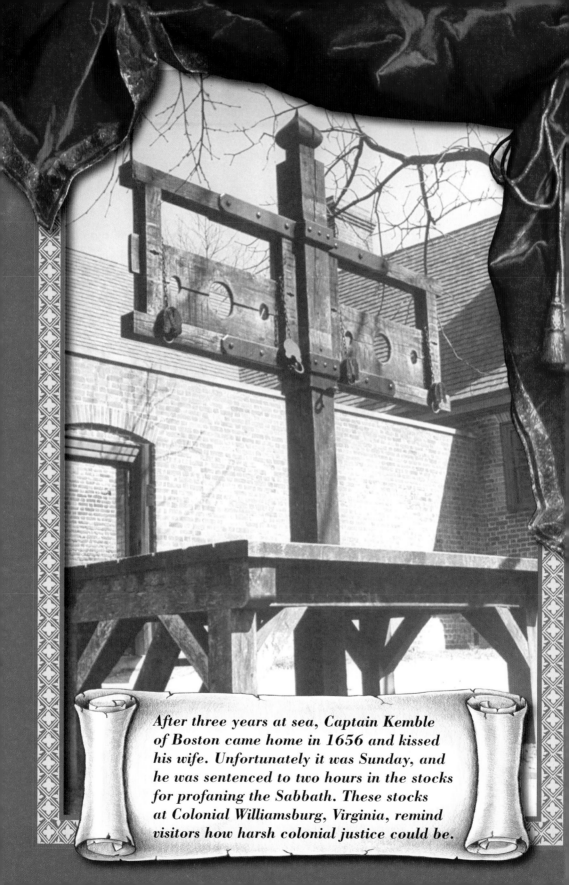

After three years at sea, Captain Kemble of Boston came home in 1656 and kissed his wife. Unfortunately it was Sunday, and he was sentenced to two hours in the stocks for profaning the Sabbath. These stocks at Colonial Williamsburg, Virginia, remind visitors how harsh colonial justice could be.

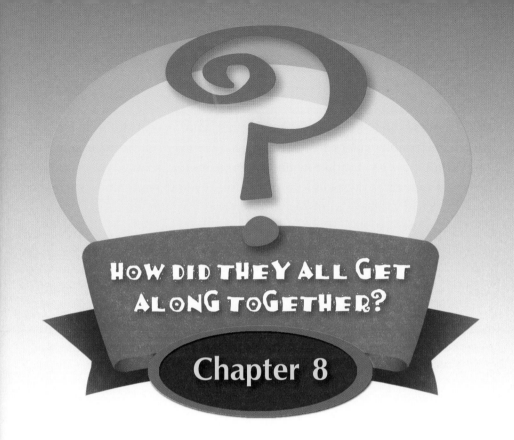

HOW DID THEY ALL GET ALONG TOGETHER?

Chapter 8

People in Colonial America represented an amazing variety of cultures. Native Americans from dozens of tribes, Europeans from many nations, and Africans from several areas of the African continent all had their own language and traditions. They did not always get along. Conflicts could be violent. Victors were often cruel toward losers. Political power rested in the hands of a few men, and the laws did not treat everyone equally. But most people did strive to live together in peace. A few had even begun to think of society in new ways and wonder what words like *freedom* and *justice* could really mean.

CRIME AND PUNISHMENT

In colonial America, laws governed every aspect of life. People did not have the freedoms they do today. They could be arrested for cursing, speaking disrespectfully of their neighbors, failing to attend church on Sunday, or simply being idle. People convicted of minor crimes were usually sentenced to the stocks. Culprits sat with their hands and feet, and sometimes head, locked in a wooden frame for as long as an entire day. Passers-by felt free to toss mud, eggs, and animal dung at the unfortunate troublemakers to insure they were even more miserable.

Whipping was another common punishment. Convicted criminals were sentenced to a specific number of strokes, sometimes so many that they had to be administered in several installments over a period of days or weeks. Repeat offenders could be branded with a hot iron as well as whipped.

Though colonial justice may seem harsh to us, it is important to remember that it was not as brutal as that in Europe, where offenders could be executed for any of a slew of minor crimes. In America, everyone's labor contributed to the community, so capital punishment was reserved for the most serious offenses, such as murder and treason. Jail sentences tended to be short. Those convicted of lesser crimes were expected to take their punishment and then get back to work.

LAW AND ORDER

Colonial society placed great emphasis on obedience to authority. Children were supposed to obey their parents; wives, their husbands; servants, apprentices, and slaves, their masters. Everybody was expected to obey the governors appointed by the British Crown.

A limited form of democracy existed in New England, where town meetings could be called to decide local issues. But only white men with property could vote at these meetings. Men without property, women, children, indentured servants, Native Americans, and African Americans had virtually no say in the laws that governed them.

Does that mean they were silent? Not necessarily. People without official power could still make their voices heard through stories, songs, and arts and crafts. They may not have been able to shape the laws, but they did shape the culture and society in which everyone lived.

Colonial society encompassed many different ethnicities, social classes, and religions. Never before in history had so many different peoples come together in one land. Their lives were not always peaceful, nor did they enjoy equality and individual liberty. By its very diversity, however, colonial America forced people to think of themselves and others in new ways, a process that continues to this day.

FYInfo

Anne Hutchinson: Champion of Women's Rights and Freedom of Religion

In 1637, the trial of a forty-six-year-old housewife named Anne Hutchinson plunged Puritan Massachusetts into an uproar.

What had she done? She had said that women should be equal to men. Even more scandalous, she opposed blind obedience to the church, believing people should follow their own conscience in spiritual matters. Every week people met at her house to hear her speak, and many of them had started to agree with her "radical" notions.

Trial of Anne Hutchinson

Alarmed, the clergy had her arrested and charged with heresy, a crime punishable by death. They called her ideas "abominable" and unnatural. At her trial, however, Anne answered their questions so clearly and cleverly, they could not make the charges stick. Instead of executing her, the court sentenced her to banishment.

Fortunately, Anne and her family found refuge in nearby Rhode Island, where she continued to spread her controversial theories.

In 1922, Massachusetts erected a memorial statue to its former rebel, honoring her as a "courageous exponent of civil liberty and religious toleration." Today, she is acknowledged as a role model for human rights activists throughout the world.

HOW TO MAKE YOUR OWN HORN BOOK

In colonial times, hornbooks were sometimes called battledores because they looked like the paddle in the game battledore and shuttlecock, which was played like today's badminton. Making your own hornbook from cardboard can be a fun way to practice your penmanship and display a personal motto, slogan, or poem.

Here is what you need:
- A pencil
- Heavy-duty, stiff poster board or cardboard
- A strong pair of scissors. If you have adult help, you can also use a box-cutter.
- A sheet of unlined white paper, 8 1/2" x 11", plus a few sheets on which to practice
- A ruler. If you want to make lines the colonial way, use a string with a weight at the end of it.
- A pen. Using a fountain pen is very authentic, but any favorite pen that allows you to write smoothly will do.
- Spray adhesive or glue
- A sheet of clear, self-adhesive acetate a little larger than your paper. You can find this in art supply or craft stores. If you don't have any, strong plastic wrap and clear tape will do.
- Aluminum foil
- A string or ribbon to loop through the handle

Instructions
1   Hornbooks came in many sizes, but making a nice, large one will give you plenty of room to write. Using your ruler, mark off a rectangle on the poster board, 10" x 12 ". (This is about the same size as a large manila envelope.) Don't cut it yet. You need a handle.

2   At the bottom of your rectangle, attach a smaller rectangle, about 4 inches wide and 5 inches long. If you want to be fancy, you can make it a little narrower at the top or round off the bottom.

3   Cut very carefully around the complete pattern. Set your cardboard hornbook aside.

4   Using your ruler (or string) and a very light pencil, mark off lines on the paper. You want your writing to be seen, so don't make the lines too close. At least ½ inch apart should do.

5   Now it's time to get creative. What do you want on your hornbook? Here are some of the traditional things: the alphabet in both capital and small letters; numerals from 1 to 9; punctuation symbols; arithmetic signs; a short verse, poem, story, prayer, paragraph, or a few aphorisms (remember *Poor Richard's Almanack*) that are meaningful to you.

6   On your practice sheets, write everything out the way you want it to look.

7   When you are satisfied, copy it on your lined sheet.

8   Glue your sheet to one side of your hornbook.

9   Take the self-adhesive acetate and very carefully cover the paper. As an alternative, you can wrap your hornbook in plastic wrap, and tape the wrap, to protect it.

10 The most elaborate hornbooks were edged with silver. You can use aluminum foil to edge yours.

11 With the tip of the scissors, push a hole through the handle. If the cardboard is very stiff, ask an adult to do this for you.

12 Run a string or ribbon through the hole and tie it in a loop for easy carrying.

Hornbooks make nice gifts. You can personalize them for your friends and family by adding a recipe, song, or even pictures. Use your imagination!

1492	Christopher Columbus sails from Spain to the Caribbean Islands.
1497	John Cabot claims the northeast coast of Canada for England.
1507	The name America is first used, referring to the Italian mapmaker and navigator Amerigo Vespucci.
1519–1522	Ferdinand Magellan sails around the world.
1565	St. Augustine, the first European settlement in North America, is established by the Spanish in Florida.
1587	The first English colony is founded in Roanoke, Virginia. On August 18, Virginia Dare is born. The colony disappears over the winter. Its fate is not known.
1607	The English colony of Jamestown is founded in Virginia. The winter, known as the starving time, reduces their number to only 35 individuals. Chief Powhatan comes to their assistance, and eventually the colony begins to thrive.
1609	Henry Hudson sails up the Hudson River as far as the present city of Albany, New York.
1619	Twenty Africans are brought to Jamestown. They are treated as indentured servants, but by 1640 most Africans in the colonies have become slaves.
1620	The English ship *The Mayflower*, carrying a group of Puritans, lands on Cape Cod. The colony is named Plymouth and becomes the first town in Massachusetts.
1623	New Hampshire is founded by James Wheelwright.
1626	The Dutch, led by Peter Minuit, believe they buy Manhattan from Native Americans for the equivalent of $24. They name their settlement New Amsterdam.
1630	The city of Boston is founded by John Winthrop.
1634	First Catholics arrive in America and found the colony of Maryland under the sponsorship of Lord Baltimore.
1635	Boston Latin School becomes the first public school in America. It accepts only boys. James Hooker founds Connecticut.
1636	Harvard College is founded. Roger Williams founds Rhode Island.
1637	Anne Hutchinson is exiled from Massachusetts because of her religious views; she founds a settlement with her family in Rhode Island.
1638	First printing press in the colonies is installed in a shop in Cambridge, Massachusetts. Peter Minuit and the New Sweden Company found Delaware.
1652	Rhode Island passes the first colonial law against slavery.

1663	King Charles of England establishes the colony of Carolina and gives the land to his supporters.
1675–1676	King Philip's War between the English colonists and Native American nations ends with a victory for the colonists.
1681	Pennsylvania is founded by William Penn, a Quaker.
1682	First immigrants from Germany arrive in Pennsylvania.
1688	Pennsylvania Quakers issue a proclamation protesting slavery.
1692	Salem holds its witch trials. Over the summer, 150 people are accused of witchcraft. Twenty are executed. The court is dissolved by October. After this, there are no more large-scale witchcraft trials in the colonies.
1699	The city of Williamsburg becomes the capital of Virginia.
1704	First newspaper in the colonies, *The Boston Newsletter*, begins publication.
1706	Benjamin Franklin is born in Boston.
1710	The British establish a postal system in the American colonies.
1712	Carolina is divided into North and South. Pennsylvania bans the importation of slaves.
1714	Tea is imported to the colonies for the first time.
1729	City of Baltimore is founded in Maryland.
1731	Benjamin Franklin founds America's first public library in Philadelphia.
1733	Georgia, founded by James Oglethorpe, becomes the last of the thirteen original colonies.
1734–1735	John Peter Zenger, a printer in New York, is accused of sedition and later acquitted. His trial becomes a milestone in the establishment of laws protecting free speech.
1737	Connecticut becomes the first colony to mint money.
1751	First municipal hospital is founded in Philadelphia.
1753	Benjamin Franklin and William Hunter become the first postmasters general overseeing mail in the colonies.
1754–1763	French and Indian War is fought between English and French forces. George Washington emerges as a leader of the colonial forces. The English victory gives England control of the thirteen colonies along the eastern seaboard from Maine to Georgia.
1776	Colonists declare independence from Great Britain.

PHOTO CREDITS: Cover, p. 1 John Durand, *The Rapalje Children*—New-York Historical Society; pp. 6–7, 10, 16, 43—Library of Congress; pp. 14, 22—Barbara Marvis; p. 18—David Walbert/by-nc-sa-2.5; p. 19—Brother O'Mara/by-nc-nd-2.0; p. 28—Wallyg/by-nc-nd-2.0; p. 36—*New England Primer*; p. 46—Bill Barber/by-nc-2.0; p. 52—*Time Inc.* Every effort has been made to locate all copyright holders of material used in this book. If any errors or omissions have occurred, corrections will be made in future editions of the book.

Books

Alexrod-Contrada, Joan. *A Historical Atlas of Colonial America.* New York: Rosen, 2005.

Giblin, James. *The Amazing Life of Benjamin Franklin.* New York: Scholastic, 2000.

Roberts, Russell. *Holidays and Celebrations in Colonial America.* Hockessin, DE: Mitchell Lane Publishers, 2007.

Studelska, Jane V. *Women of Colonial America.* Minneapolis, MN: Compass Point Books, 2007.

Works Consulted

Beatty, Barbara. *Preschool Education in America: The Culture of Young Children from the Colonial Era to the Present.* New Haven: Yale University Press, 1995.

Belote, Julianne. *The Compleat American Housewife, 1776.* Concord, CA: Nitty Gritty Productions, 1974.

Bradford, William; edited by William T. Davis. Bradford's *History of Plymouth Plantation, 1606-1646.* New York: Barnes & Noble, 1959.

Bremner, Robert Hamlett. *Children and Youth in America: A Documentary History.* Cambridge, MA: Harvard University Press, 1970–74.

Earle, Alice Morse. *Child Life in Colonial Days.* New York: Macmillan, 1927.

Franklin, Benjamin. *The Autobiography.* New York: Vintage Books/Library of America, 1990.

Franklin, Benjamin. *Poor Richard's Almanack; Being the Almanacks of 1733, 1749, 1756, 1757, 1758.* Garden City, NY: Doubleday, Doran and Company, Inc., 1928.

Grant, Anne MacVicar. *Memoirs of an American Lady, with Sketches of Manners and Scenes in America as They Existed Previous to the Revolution.* Albany, NY: J. Munsell, 1876.

Hands On History, Inc., Colonial American Fair: Cooking Recipes http://www.handsonhistoryinc.org/HOH-Page11.html

Holliday, Carl. *Woman's Life in Colonial Days.* Williamstown, MA: Corner House Publishers, 1968.

Marten, James. *Children in Colonial America.* New York: New York University Press, 2007.

Plimpton, George A. *The Hornbook and Its Use in America.* Worcester, MA: American Antiquarian Society, 1916.

Rath, Richard Cullen. *How Early America Sounded.* Ithaca, NY: Cornell University Press, 2003.

Reiss, Oscar. *Medicine in Colonial America.* Lanham, MD: University Press of America, 2000.

Simmons, Amelia. *The First American Cookbook: A Facsimile of "American Cookery," 1796,* with an Essay by Mary Tolford Wilson. New York: Dover Publications, 1984.

Smith, Helen Evertson. *Colonial Days and Ways, as Gathered from Family Papers.* New York: Ungar, 1966.

Tittle, Walter. *Colonial Holidays.* New York: Doubleday, Page & Co., 1910.

Wilbur, C. Keith. *Home Building and Woodworking in Colonial America.* Old Saybrook, CT: Globe Pequot Press, 1992.

Worrell, Estelle Ansley. *Children's Costume in America, 1607–1910.* New York: Scribner, 1980.

On the Internet

Colonial Kids: A Celebration of Life in the 1700s
http://library.thinkquest.org/J002611F/

Colonial Williamsburg
http://www.history.org

Jamestown Settlement
http://www.historyisfun.org

Library of Congress: Colonial America 1492–1763
http://www.americaslibrary.gov/cgi-bin/page.cgi/jb/colonial

Plimoth Plantation
http://www.plimoth.org

Strawbery Banke, Portsmouth, New Hampshire
http://www.strawberybanke.org

GLOSSARY

adze—A tool shaped like a small hoe, with a sharp, curved blade used for scraping wood.

aphorism (AA-for-ih-zum)—A short, pithy observation that contains a general truth.

apothecary (uh-PAH-thuh-kayr-ee)—A person trained to prepare and sell medicines.

apprentice (uh-PREN-tiss)—Someone, usually a young person, who has agreed to learn a trade from a skilled employer for a fixed period and who works for little or no pay.

breeches (BRIT-chis)—Short trousers that reach just below the knee.

cabinetmaker (KAB-nit-may-ker)—A skilled furniture maker.

codfish—A large fish common in the North Atlantic used for both food and oil.

common—A piece of open land or pasture set aside for public use in a village or town.

contra dance (KON-truh dahnts)—A traditional English dance in which couples form lines facing each other.

cooper—A barrel maker.

cornmeal—A coarse flour made by grinding dried corn kernels.

distaff—A stick that holds wool for spinning.

Dutch oven—A large, deep pot with a close-fitting lid used for cooking.

felling ax—An ax with a heavy head and sharp curved blade used for chopping down trees.

flax—A tall, fibrous, reedlike plant used for making linen.

hornbook—A wooden slate with the alphabet on one side used to teach young children how to read.

indentured servant—Someone who agrees to work for a period of time in order to repay his or her employer for transportation to the employer's country and related costs.

liaison (LEE-ay-zon)—A person who helps different groups get along together, often by interpreting language.

leads, or lead strings—Strings attached to the back of a small child's dress that could be held to keep the child from wandering away.

magistrate (MAA-jih-strayt)—An officer of the law who can also act as judge in minor court cases.

militia (mih-LIH-shuh)—A volunteer military force.

milliner (MIH-lih-ner)—A maker of women's hats.

moccasin (MAH-kuh-sin)—A soft-soled slip-on shoe originally made by Native Americans.

musket—A gun with a long barrel, loaded from the front of the barrel.

petticoat (PEH-tih-koht)—A slip or underskirt worn by women and girls.

pewter (PYOO-tur)—A soft metal made of tin and copper, or tin and lead, used for small items such as jewelry and tableware.

pinafore (PIH-nuh-for)—A low-necked piece of clothing—either long like a dress or shorter, like an apron—that is worn over other garments.

pudding cap—A padded cap worn by babies and toddlers to protect their head.

scurvy—A disease that weakens the skin, caused by the lack of vitamin C.

silversmith—One who works with silver.

spinning wheel—A wooden wheel on a frame used to spin thread or yarn.

stays—A corset made in two separate pieces, laced together and reinforced by flexible wood or whalebone, worn by women and girls.

stocks—A punishment device consisting of a solid wood frame with holes in which a person's hands, feet, and head can be locked.

tinderbox—A metal box containing material for kindling a fire, including flint, steel, and a piece of charred fabric or wood.

trencher—A shallow wooden bowl or a piece of bread that serves as a bowl.

trundle bed—A small, low bed that can be stored under a larger bed.

ABOUT THE AUTHOR

A former history major, Patrice Sherman has worked as an archivist for several museum and university libraries and is especially interested in social and cultural history. She is the author of several children's books, including Class Trip to Boston *for Mitchell Lane Publishers. In addition, her articles have been published in the magazine* Learning Through History, *and she produced* Growing Up at Work: A History of Child Labor in America, *a multimedia educational program for the Massachusetts History Workshop. Sherman lives in Cambridge, Massachusetts.*